THE BOOK
OF PRAISES

תהלים

TRANSLATIONS FROM THE PSALMS

C000281325

THE BOOK
OF PRAISES

TRANSLATIONS FROM THE PSALMS

R O G E R W A G N E R

CANTERBURY
PRESS

Norwich

© Roger Wagner 2020

First published in 2020 by the Canterbury Press Norwich
Editorial office
3rd Floor, Invicta House
108–114 Golden Lane
London EC1Y 0TG, UK
www.canterburypress.co.uk

Canterbury Press is an imprint of Hymns Ancient & Modern Ltd
(a registered charity)

Hymns Ancient & Modern® is a registered trademark of
Hymns Ancient & Modern Ltd
13A Hellesdon Park Road, Norwich,
Norfolk NR6 5DR, UK

All rights reserved. No part of this publication may be reproduced,
stored in a retrieval system, or transmitted,
in any form or by any means, electronic, mechanical,
photocopying or otherwise, without the prior permission of
the publisher, Canterbury Press.

The Author has asserted his right under the Copyright, Designs and Patents Act 1988
to be identified as the Author of this Work

British Library Cataloguing in Publication data

A catalogue record for this book is available
from the British Library

978-1-78622-284-8

Printed and bound in Great Britain by
Bell & Bain, Glasgow

Acknowledgements

Since the inception of this (still unfinished) project there has been a long procession of people who have helped it along its way and to whom thanks are due. It starts with Dr Jeremy Hughes who first allowed me to join his Hebrew class at the Oxford Jewish Studies Centre and later his Biblical Hebrew reading class at the Oriental Institute, and immediately continues with the late Professor Edward Ullendorff who read my first translations and gave me the courage to proceed.

Book One would nevertheless not have appeared without the help of Dr Christian Brady who spent endless hours fitting the Hebrew text around the engravings, and Bex Marriott who designed the cover and made the books. All of the first three books were printed at the Senecio Press and I am very grateful to the care and skill of the Lack family, Adrian, Andrea, Alexander and Amelia, who variously helped with the production of the first three books and the formatting of images for the present one. Similarly I am very grateful to Judith Fisher, for her work on the typesetting of the present book, and to Mary Matthews, Stephen Rogers and Christine Smith from Canterbury Press for all their work on it.

The idea for this present selection I owe the to Oxford Torch Psalms Project, and in particular to Professor Susan Gillingham and Dr Danny Crowther. It was the latter who alerted me to the misplaced cantillation marks that I had included in two of the earlier books and guided me in their removal. I am also very grateful to Dr Peter Southwell for reading through and alerting me to some omissions in the text. It must be stressed however that none of the distinguished Hebrew scholars mentioned above bears the slightest blame for any of the errors, omissions or strained translations that may remain, for all of which I take full responsibility.

Introduction

Sometime in the early nineties I was staying with some friends in Sheffield. While waiting for them to return, I started exploring their bookshelves and came across an old leather bound confirmation present. This was *A Book of Psalms*: Ronald Knox's translation of the psalter. Although I didn't get on with the translation, as I sat waiting, the idea of a different kind of book of psalms began to take shape in my mind.

Many years earlier, while still at school, I had visited the convent of San Marco in Florence where in each of the friars' cells there is a painting by Fra Angelico illustrating some episode from the gospels. Sitting in those cells had been a formative part of my own spiritual journey and had shown me at the same time how paintings could speak to deep places in the soul.

That experience in Florence had shaped my own ambition as a painter, but while painting had been at the centre of my life I had also had a longstanding interest in poetry. After I left art school and moved up to Oxford I started writing some poetry and produced some illustrated books in which I tried to combine the two things. The same literary interest had led me to join Dr Jeremy Hughes' class in biblical Hebrew which (it being Oxford) I discovered was taking place just down the road from my studio.

As I sat looking through Ronald Knox's psalm book in Sheffield all these various experiences began to come together. Because the psalms are so various and different from each other – speaking to every mood and shift in our spiritual weather – reading through the psalter can feel like walking through a spacious building in which each poem, like the individual cells in San Marco, provides an opportunity for contemplation and reflection. Might it be possible to produce a book of psalms that attempted something like this, where a fresh translation of each psalm appeared alongside an illustration that invited the reader to pause and contemplate some aspect of it?

To read the poems that we call 'psalms' is in fact to enter into the life of an actual building (though one that was first destroyed some two and a half thousand years ago).

The temple in Jerusalem carved throughout with 'cherubim, palm trees and open flowers', with its interior 'from wall to floor overlaid with gold' was the backdrop (as numerous references within the psalms make clear) against which these poems were originally performed. The Greek word *psalmos* refers to the music of a stringed instrument or to a song sung to this accompaniment, and it is clear (again from multiple references within them) that the psalms were songs intended for performance by temple singers and musicians.

The physical destruction of the temple ('with axes and hatchets/they hack away all the engraved work'[1]) together with the abolition of its musical life and the dispersal of musicians and choirs, left the psalms orphaned from their parent culture. In doing so however, it also made them a unique seed of human creativity. Perhaps no other collection of poems in the history of the world has drawn out such a range and depth of imaginative responses.

In reading the psalms we in a sense recreate the life of the temple, so that with each new reading the walls of the place once left desolate are, stone by stone (within the inner being of the reader), imaginatively rebuilt. But the creativity these poems inspired went beyond mere imagination.

The orphan status of the psalms is nowhere more clearly indicated than in their titles. It is these which remind us that the psalms are songs for which we have the words but not the music. 'Lillies', 'alamoth', 'doves of far off terebinths', 'do not

---

1 Psalm 74

destroy', 'hind of the dawn', probably all refer to settings and tunes. Likewise the so-called technical terms *higgaion, sheminith, maskil, selah,* were presumably intended to give some kind of guide to performance, but it is not clear that even the Jewish Septuagint translators knew exactly what all these archaic terms referred to.

For the psalms to be used – to be sung in the synagogue, to be sung by Jesus and his disciples, to be sung by the early church – new music and new settings were required. The first seed of creativity that the psalms sowed, both in second temple and later Judaism and in the early church, was consequently a musical one.

And accompanying the seed of music was a seed of poetry. As the psalms moved out from their original context into the Jewish diaspora and into the early church communities they were translated (along with the rest of the scriptures) first into Greek, then into Latin and Coptic and eventually into innumerable other languages.

Robert Frost famously defined poetry as 'that which is lost in translation'. Frost may overstate the case, but while all translation is problematic, translating the heightened speech of poetry into another language does involve particular challenges.

The characteristic of the psalms that the 18th century Anglican Bishop Robert Lowth first described as 'parallelism' (saying something and then repeating it in different words) is a poetic technique, which as C S Lewis pointed out, survives translation in way that metre and rhyme can't. Other aspects of their poetry though are more evanescent. From the first line of the first psalm *'ashre ha'ish 'asher lo halakh ba'tsath rsha'im* we are presented with a mouthful of subtly rhyming vowels and consonants that inevitably evaporate in translation. So do the alphabetical acrostics. So do the particular cultural resonances of the psalmist's imagery.

Any translator who is to do justice to their task, is thus faced with finding a poetic idiom, an equivalent verbal music or heightened speech within the language of their own place and time. The translator must become a poet.

The title of this collection of poems in the Hebrew bible is *Sepher Tehillim* – 'The Book of Praises', and praise is the *cantus firmus* the 'fixed song' that sounds throughout the collection. The five books of 150 psalms have in consequence provided Jews and Christians over the centuries with something like a language of thanksgiving: a vocabulary of gratitude.

If though praise is the 'fixed song' of the collection, it is surrounded by a counterpoint of other voices. These are voices of complaint, lament, and anger: expressions of pain, of guilt, of spiritual desolation and longing. They contradict, challenge and interrogate the larger theme, indeed sometimes seem on the point (though that point is never quite reached) of overwhelming the unshakeable *cantus firmus* of the whole collection.

Although the psalms sometimes speak to and with the voice of a whole community, in very many of the psalms the tone is highly personal. Consequently the rapid alternation between the antiphonal voices of complaint, lamentation or violent anger and the *cantus firmus* of praise, often seem to reflect the sudden changes of spiritual weather that occur within the inner life of an individual.

All these *dramatis personae* need to be heard. The translator must become not only a poet but a dramatist.

Nevertheless however poignant the personal situations out of which the psalms seem to spring, the performance notes and the existence of the collection itself, makes clear that these individual voices have been folded into the worship of the community of Israel as it comes to the house of the Lord where the golden cherubim symbolise the abiding presence of God.

If the requirements of singing and reading made the psalms a seed of music and poetry, it was this need to imaginatively recreate some equivalent to the temple setting that made the psalms a seed of visual creativity. The first and most obvious form this took was in the architecture and decoration of places of worship.

The wonderful painted synagogue and the humbler painted house church at Dura Europos (both built sometime before 256 AD) were early instalments of an ever-expanding project in which new outposts of the vanished temple began to be established (often from the 5th century onwards adorned with angels standing within golden mosaics) in centres of population across the face of the known world.

The coming of a new invention, the codex or book, allowed this project to expand still further, and allowed the psalms to move outside places of public worship into the private space of personal devotion.

In this space music was left behind, but instead the text could itself become an object of patient meditation. The earliest example of a complete book of psalms or 'psalter' was found in a poor Coptic cemetery in a shallow grave placed under a young girl's head. The Mudil codex, a Coptic translation from the late 4th century, is undecorated text, but in time the script itself began to be used as a kind of musical setting: inviting the reader to pause, to linger, to enter into the meaning.

In scholars' bibles, where Jerome's four different translations appeared as parallel texts, this only involved the initial letter appearing in a different colour, but over the centuries this developed into chrysography – writing in gold – where decorated intials or even occasionally whole texts might be written in gold. From the 7th and 8th centuries, the first of what was to become a long tradition of illustrated psalters began to appear.

In church buildings any kind of imagery is a background, while liturgy, like the singing of the psalms, is enacted in front of it. In an illustrated gospel or psalter, whatever the role of the image it was still the text that needed to be in the foreground, and medieval psalm illustrators often confined their work to the margins.

When I first began translating and illustrating the psalms in the early nineteen nineties it was this relationship of text and image that was the first thing I had to think about. At the outset of the collection **Psalm 1** talks of the man whose delight is in the law of the LORD and who 'meditates', or more literally 'murmurs', his law day and night. If the purpose of illustrating the psalms was to provide a way of fixing the attention that aided this kind of 'murmuring' or 'meditation' in a private setting (where music wasn't available), it had to involve both image and text.

The late Jonathan Sachs, the former Chief Rabbi, once wrote about the different parts of the brain involved in languages that read from the right and from the left. This characteristic of English and Hebrew, suggested a way in which the placing of both images and text could express the meaning of the poems.

Thus in **Psalm 1** the two ways set out by the psalmist are echoed in the two blocks of text and their accompanying images. In **Psalms 3 and 4** which both allude to the rhythm of waking and sleeping, the placing of the images echo that rhythm. In **Psalm 5** the way the text surrounds the image, echoes the way in the illustration the angel's wings surround the man, which in turn is echoing the final line of the psalm 'you surround them with acceptance as with a great shield'. In **Psalm 6** the disturbance of the first part of the poem 'my soul is much troubled' is matched by a disturbed interlacing of the English and Hebrew which then resolves into a calmer conclusion: 'the LORD has heard the sound of my weeping'. In **Psalm 8** the blocks of text are shaped like a chalice or outspread hands mirroring the poem's theme of wonder. In **Psalm 29** which begins with inviting the sons of God to give glory to the LORD and goes on to speak of the voice of the LORD being 'over the waters', the English and Hebrew are shaped into a wing formation. In **Psalm 38** where desolation predominates, the whole psalm is a disturbed interlace.

By 2008 when I translated and illustrated the second book of psalms (42-72), the development of digital printing had made it possible to follow the mediaeval psalters and introduce coloured images. That immediately brought with it new ways of expressing the meaning of the text. So in **Psalms 42** and **43** the psalmist's disturbed dialogue with himself 'why are you oppressed O my soul?' is accompanied by a repeated black and white image of a divided mind which finally resolves into single figure in a world where colour has returned. In **Psalm 49** the surrounding black and white wood engraving expresses the pervasive theme that 'wise men die, the stupid and the brutal/together perish' , while the small colour image at the centre asserts the opposite hope 'that God will redeem my life from the hand of death'.

Colour in its nature detains the eye, and produces a focus of meditation without the need for expressive text. So that while occasionally as in **Psalm 51** the Hebrew and English text are in the same way interlaced to express the poet's anguish, more often in this book the Hebrew text appears only to accent words or phrases and to frame the illustrations.

The psalms in this present volume are selected from the first three books of the psalter, and in each of these books the relationship between illustration and psalm can take a variety of forms. Occasionally where the centre of the psalm is the reminiscence of a particular historical moment, a natural way of illustration is to try and make that moment more vivid. In **Psalm 66** where the text describes how 'he turned the sea into dry land, they passed through the river on foot ...we went through fire and water but you brought us out into freedom', the image is therefore of crossing the red sea. In **Psalm 18** where David's deliverance from the hand of his enemies is described both in terms of a physical battle and in the language of God's coming down to earth, the image tries to combine these two perspectives.

More often though I found that the illustrations were picking up something within the imagery of the psalm. In **Psalm 6** for instance 'the LORD has heard the sound of my weeping' this was the imagery of God as a parent. When it came to the lines in **Psalm 8** which describe how 'Out of the mouths of children and suckling babies/You have founded a stronghold of praise' and goes on to talk of looking 'at your heavens/The work of your fingers/The moon and the stars which you created', I found myself reminded of Newton's description of himself as being like a little child playing with shining pebbles on a beach while the great ocean of truth lay all undiscovered before him.

The imagery of water which flows through a number of the psalms also finds its way into a number of the illustrations. Thus in **Psalm 42** which begins by describing how 'As a hind yearns for water/So my soul/Yearns for you/O God', and goes on to articulate how when the psalmist's 'soul is very oppressed' he remembers how 'From the mountain of Mijar/Deep calls unto deep/In the roar of your cataracts', the waterfall continues through the psalm and on into the illustration of **Psalm 43**. The declaration in **Psalm 46** that 'There is a river/Whose streams make glad/The city of God' is not intended to be literal (there is no river in Jerusalem), and the ideal river depicted is borrowed from Piero della Francesca. The statement on the other hand in **Psalm 65** that 'The river of God/Is full of water' is connected with the actual fruitfulness of the earth and brought to mind an Oxfordshire harvest.

It has been said of Shakespeare's plays that they have been transfigured by their history. Originally the product of a single mind, as countless other minds have poured their thoughts and emotions into them, they have become 'full of quotations'. That must inevitably be even more true of sacred texts like the psalms, so that it is hardly possible to hear the opening lines of **Psalm** 22 for instance without hearing their quotation on the lips of Christ.

The relationship between the psalms and the Gospel stories however goes far deeper than simply that of quotation.

The story at the end of Luke's gospel, in which a stranger (the as yet unrecognised risen Jesus) walks with two disciples along the road to Emmaus, describes how 'beginning with Moses and all prophets, he explained to them what was said in all the scriptures concerning himself'. The implication of this story - that 'in all the scriptures' there is a message about Jesus - is exactly the perspective of the beginning of the letter to the Hebrews where the author sites a whole series of verses from the psalms, claiming that God is speaking these verses 'about the son'.

Likewise in the gospels themselves Jesus is represented not only as claiming that 'Moses wrote these things about me', but implying that David in the psalms had done the same. Thus he sites verses from psalm 110 as referring to himself, while the gospel writers site verses referring to the figure of the sufferer in the psalms as prophecies that Jesus would fulfil.

The Emmaus story in Luke's gospel describes the culminating moment, when old texts suddenly becoming transparent to a new kind of meaning, in graphically visual terms. The disciples' hearts may have burned within them while they listened to Jesus opening up the scriptures to them, but it is as they watch him breaking bread that 'their eyes were opened and they recognised him'.

Whereas music and words take time, visual images travel at the speed of light and from our perspective are instantaneous. From their first appearance in Christian buildings it seems to have been recognised that visual images were perfectly adapted to the revelation of this kind of multiple meaning. Thus in the earliest dateable Christian church, the house church at Dura Europos, there is a painting of a shepherd with a flock of sheep, one of whom seems to be drinking from a stream. This can naturally be seen as an illustration of Psalm 23 – the LORD is my shepherd. Yet because it stands above a Christian baptistery it is also, and at exactly the same moment, an image of Christ as the good shepherd and of us as the lost sheep.

In the first illustrated psalters there is often an image of David set alongside an image of Christ. For many of the psalms, gospel stories provide an illustration because the psalm and the story can be seen to occupy the same space.

Thus when **Psalm 44** says 'Wake up! Why do you sleep Lord?', it uses more or less the same language as the disciples addressing Jesus sleeping in the boat on the lake of Galilee. When **Psalm 77** says 'Your path/is in the sea/Your road/is in/the great waters' it might be describing Jesus walking on the lake. When **Psalm 49** says that 'God will redeem my life from the hand of death' it could be offering a commentary on the raising of Lazarus. When **Psalm 79** says 'let your compassion/come quickly/to meet us/for we are brought/very low', it might be describing the meeting of the prodigal son and his father. When **Psalm 73** concludes 'as for me/the closeness of God/is my/good', these could be the words spoken by Simeon in the temple when he takes the Christ child in his arms.

The conclusion of **Psalm 73** comes at the very end of a lament in which the *cantus firmus* of praise has come very close to being overwhelmed by negative emotions, 'For my heart was embittered/I was like a brute/I knew nothing/I was a behemoth before you', and it is followed by **Psalm 74** where the destruction of the temple for the first time comes into view: 'They set your holy place/on fire/They defiled/The dwelling place/of your name/in the dust'.

In the final book of the psalter, psalm 137 records how after the temple's destruction, the Jewish exiles in Babylon were asked for songs by their captors 'sing us one from the "the songs of Sion"'. Their reply is a question 'how shall we sing the LORD's song in a strange land?', which is asking how these songs could possibly make sense outside the context in which they were written and for which they were created.

Psalm 137 with its deep lament and terrible ending is itself more 'a song of Babylon' than 'a song of Sion'. And yet in finding language to express its sorrow and rage and to recall all that has been lost, it does in a sense answer its own question and becomes a new kind of 'song of Sion'. In doing so it both models and exemplifies the way that both the psalms and psalm singing have a capacity to step outside their original context into the situation of other times.

In this selection from the first three books of psalms it is only the illustration to **Psalm** 53 that does this in a literal sense. The psalm begins 'The fool said in his heart:/ "there is no God"/they corrupted themselves/they performed an abominable evil', and in psalm 14 which is more or less identical I illustrated this with an image of the flood. But in **Psalm** 53 when I came to the lines 'shall not all who do evil/be made to know it./They consume my people/as they consume bread/they do not call upon God', the only appropriate illustration seemed to be an image that recalled the holocaust.

Yet even this bleakest of visions ends, as do many of the psalms, with an exhortation to rejoice: 'When God/brings his people home/let Jacob rejoice/let Israel be glad'. To find some visual equivalent to the celebration of the presence of God, which is the *cantus firmus* of the whole collection, I found myself constantly returning to the golden cherubim 'carved throughout the temple' which were the backdrop against which the psalms were originally sung.

Thus in **Psalm** 5 the idea of entering God's house is suggested by the presence of an angel. In **Psalm** 19 the sun like a bridegroom coming forth from his marriage tent becomes an angelic version of Blake's *Glad Day* while **Psalm** 30 includes an angelic version of his *Death's Door*. In **Psalm 60** God tossing his sandal over Edom is represented as a giant 'angel of the LORD', while in **Psalm 85** faithfulness springing up from the earth and righteousness leaning down from heaven becomes two embracing angels.

Finally in this selection, the universal vision of **Psalm 87** in which the traditional enemies of Israel 'Babel … Philstia and Tyre together with Cush' are recorded 'as those that know me' and where of 'Sion (mother)/it will be said /each and everyone/is born in her', flights of angels, like the cherubim in the temple, fill every available space.

While the physical temple may have been destroyed, that to which it bore witness remains an endless source of hope and creativity: 'So singers as dancers: "all my springs are in you"'.

אַשְׁרֵי הָאִישׁ
אֲשֶׁר לֹא הָלַךְ בַּעֲצַת רְשָׁעִים
וּבְדֶרֶךְ חַטָּאִים לֹא עָמָד
וּבְמוֹשַׁב לֵצִים לֹא יָשָׁב:
כִּי אִם בְּתוֹרַת יְהוָה חֶפְצוֹ
וּבְתוֹרָתוֹ יֶהְגֶּה יוֹמָם וָלָיְלָה:
וְהָיָה כְּעֵץ שָׁתוּל עַל־פַּלְגֵי מָיִם
אֲשֶׁר פִּרְיוֹ יִתֵּן בְּעִתּוֹ
וְעָלֵהוּ לֹא־יִבּוֹל
וְכֹל אֲשֶׁר־יַעֲשֶׂה יַצְלִיחַ:
לֹא־כֵן הָרְשָׁעִים
כִּי אִם־כַּמֹּץ אֲשֶׁר־תִּדְּפֶנּוּ רוּחַ:
עַל־כֵּן לֹא־יָקֻמוּ רְשָׁעִים בַּמִּשְׁפָּט
וְחַטָּאִים בַּעֲדַת צַדִּיקִים:
כִּי־יוֹדֵעַ יְהוָה דֶּרֶךְ צַדִּיקִים
וְדֶרֶךְ רְשָׁעִים תֹּאבֵד:

The happiness of the man
Who has not walked
In the counsel of the wicked,
And has not stood
In the path of sinners,
And has not sat
In the seat of scoffers,
But whose delight
Is in the law of the LORD
And murmurs his law day and night!
He will be like a tree planted
By rivers of water
Which gives its fruit in its time
And whose leaf does not whither
And all that he does will prosper.
Not so the wicked
They are like chaff
Which the wind will scatter
Therefore the wicked will not stand
In the judgement
Nor sinners
In the assembly of the righteous
For the LORD knows the path
Of the righteous
But the path of the wicked
Shall be lost.

ג

A Hymn of David when he fled
Before Absalom his son.

מִזְמוֹר לְדָוִד בְּבָרְחוֹ
מִפְּנֵי אַבְשָׁלוֹם בְּנוֹ:

O LORD how many have become
My enemies!
Thousands are rising against me
Thousands are saying of me
"For him there is no help in God."

יְהוָה מָה־רַבּוּ
צָרָי
רַבִּים קָמִים עָלָי:
רַבִּים אֹמְרִים לְנַפְשִׁי
אֵין יְשׁוּעָתָה לּוֹ בֵאלֹהִים

                            Selah סֶלָה:

But you LORD
Are a shield about me
My glory
And the lifter of my head!
I cry aloud to the LORD
And he has answered me
From his holy mountain.

וְאַתָּה יְהוָה
מָגֵן בַּעֲדִי
כְּבוֹדִי
וּמֵרִים רֹאשִׁי:
קוֹלִי אֶל־יְהוָה אֶקְרָא
וַיַּעֲנֵנִי מֵהַר קָדְשׁוֹ

                            Selah סֶלָה:

I lie down, I sleep
I wake up for the LORD is upholding me
I will not fear the ten thousands of people
Who have drawn up in a circle around me.
Rise up O LORD, deliver me my God!
For you have slapped all my enemies
On the cheek.
You have broken the fangs of the wicked
Salvation is from the LORD
Your blessing be upon your people.

אֲנִי שָׁכַבְתִּי וָאִישָׁנָה
הֱקִיצוֹתִי כִּי יְהוָה יִסְמְכֵנִי:
לֹא־אִירָא מֵרִבְבוֹת עָם
אֲשֶׁר סָבִיב שָׁתוּ עָלָי:
קוּמָה יְהוָה הוֹשִׁיעֵנִי אֱלֹהַי
כִּי־הִכִּיתָ אֶת־כָּל־אֹיְבַי
לֶחִי
שִׁנֵּי רְשָׁעִים שִׁבַּרְתָּ:
לַיהוָה הַיְשׁוּעָה
עַל־עַמְּךָ בִרְכָתֶךָ

                            Selah סֶלָה:

For the worship leader: with string band.
A Hymn of David.

למנצח בנגינות מזמור לדוד:

Answer me when I cry out
God of my vindication!

בקראי עני
אלהי צדק

You set me free when I was hemmed in
Have mercy on me and hear my prayer.
Sons of men how long will you
Insult my glory
Because you love emptiness
And chase after a lie.

בצר הרחבת לי
חנני ושמע תפלתי:
בני איש עד־מה
כבודי לכלמה
תאהבון ריק
תבקשו כזב

Selah: סלה

But know that the LORD has set apart
For himself the one that he loves
The LORD will hear when I cry out to him.
Shake with anger but do not sin
Speak on your bed with your own heart
And be still.

ודעו כי־הפלה יהוה
חסיד לו
יהוה ישמע בקראי אליו:
רגזו ואל־תחטאו
אמרו בלבבכם על־משכבכם
ודמו

Selah: סלה

Sacrifice righteous sacrifices
And trust in the LORD
Many are saying:
"Who will make us see prosperity?"
O LORD lift upon us
The light of your face.
You have given my heart joy
Beyond that of the time
When their corn and wine abounded.
In peace I will lie down
And sleep at once.
For you alone LORD
Make me rest without fear.

זבחו זבחי־צדק
ובטחו אל־יהוה:
רבים אמרים
מי־יראנו טוב
נסה עלינו
אור פניך יהוה:
נתתה שמחה בלבי
מעת
דגנם ותירושם רבו:
בשלום יחדו אשכבה
ואישן
כי־אתה יהוה לבדד
לבטח תושיבני:

5 For the worship leader: on flutes   לַמְנַצֵּחַ אֶל־הַנְּחִילוֹת
A Hymn of David   מִזְמוֹר לְדָוִד:
Give ear to my words O LORD   אֲמָרַי הַאֲזִינָה ׀ יְהוָה
Understand my murmuring.   בִּינָה הֲגִיגִי:
Listen out for the sound   הַקְשִׁיבָה
Of my crying for help   לְקוֹל שַׁוְעִי
My King and my God   מַלְכִּי וֵאלֹהָי
For I will pray to you,   כִּי־אֵלֶיךָ אֶתְפַּלָּל:
You will hear my voice O LORD   יְהוָה בֹּקֶר
In the morning   תִּשְׁמַע קוֹלִי
In the morning I will prepare for you   בֹּקֶר אֶעֱרָךְ־לְךָ
And keep watch.   וַאֲצַפֶּה:

For you are not a god who finds   כִּי לֹא אֵל
Pleasure in wickedness   חָפֵץ רֶשַׁע
Evil is not your guest   אָתָּה לֹא יְגֻרְךָ רָע:
The boastful shall not stand   לֹא־יִתְיַצְּבוּ הוֹלְלִים
Before your eyes.   לְנֶגֶד עֵינֶיךָ
You hate all makers of sorrow   שָׂנֵאתָ כָּל־פֹּעֲלֵי אָוֶן:
You destroy all tellers of lies   תְּאַבֵּד דֹּבְרֵי כָזָב
The LORD abhors a man of blood   אִישׁ־דָּמִים וּמִרְמָה יְתָעֵב ׀ יְהוָה:
And deception.

But I through your great love   וַאֲנִי בְּרֹב חַסְדְּךָ
Will enter your house,   אָבוֹא בֵיתֶךָ
In your awe   אֶשְׁתַּחֲוֶה
I will bow down towards your   אֶל־הֵיכַל־קָדְשְׁךָ
Holy temple   בְּיִרְאָתֶךָ:
Because they lie in wait for me   יְהוָה ׀ נְחֵנִי
Give me in your righteousness O LORD   בְצִדְקָתֶךָ לְמַעַן שׁוֹרְרָי
Make plain your way before me.   הוֹשַׁר לְפָנַי דַּרְכֶּךָ:

For in their mouth there is no honesty   כִּי אֵין בְּפִיהוּ נְכוֹנָה
Their entrails are a deep pit   קִרְבָּם הַוּוֹת
Their throat is an open grave   קֶבֶר־פָּתוּחַ גְּרוֹנָם
They make their tongue slimy   לְשׁוֹנָם יַחֲלִיקוּן:
O God pronounce them guilty   הַאֲשִׁימֵם ׀ אֱלֹהִים
Let them fall by their own counsels   יִפְּלוּ מִמֹּעֲצוֹתֵיהֶם
Throw them down in their great rebellions   בְּרֹב פִּשְׁעֵיהֶם הַדִּיחֵמוֹ
For they have rebelled against you.   כִּי־מָרוּ בָךְ:

But let all them who take refuge in you   וְיִשְׂמְחוּ
Rejoice,   כָל־חוֹסֵי בָךְ
Let them always shout for joy   לְעוֹלָם יְרַנֵּנוּ
You spread your protection over them   וְתָסֵךְ עָלֵימוֹ
And the lovers of your name   וְיַעְלְצוּ בְךָ
Exult in you.   אֹהֲבֵי שְׁמֶךָ:
For you LORD bless the righteous   כִּי־אַתָּה תְּבָרֵךְ צַדִּיק
You surround them with acceptance   יְהוָה
As with a great shield.   כַּצִּנָּה רָצוֹן תַּעְטְרֶנּוּ:

לַמְנַצֵּחַ בִּנְגִינוֹת עַל־הַשְּׁמִינִית מִזְמוֹר לְדָוִד:

For the worship leader: with string band, for bass. A hymn of David

יְהוָה אַל־בְּאַפְּךָ תוֹכִיחֵנִי וְאַל־בַּחֲמָתְךָ תְיַסְּרֵנִי:

LORD do not in your fury punish me. Do not in anger discipline me.

חָנֵּנִי יְהוָה כִּי אֻמְלַל אָנִי

LORD have mercy on me for I am weak,

רְפָאֵנִי יְהוָה כִּי נִבְהֲלוּ עֲצָמָי:

LORD heal me for my bones are troubled.

וְנַפְשִׁי נִבְהֲלָה מְאֹד וְאַתְּ יְהוָה עַד־מָתָי:

My soul is much troubled, and you O LORD how long?

שׁוּבָה יְהוָה חַלְּצָה נַפְשִׁי הוֹשִׁיעֵנִי לְמַעַן חַסְדֶּךָ:

Return O LORD, rescue my soul, save me for the sake of your love.

כִּי אֵין בַּמָּוֶת זִכְרֶךָ

For in death there is no commemoration of you;

בִּשְׁאוֹל מִי יוֹדֶה־לָּךְ:

Who gives thanks from the tomb?

יָגַעְתִּי ׀ בְּאַנְחָתִי אַשְׂחֶה בְכָל־לַיְלָה מִטָּתִי

I am worn out with groaning, and every night

בְּדִמְעָתִי עַרְשִׂי אַמְסֶה:

My bed swims, my couch melts with my tears.

עָשְׁשָׁה מִכַּעַס עֵינִי עָתְקָה בְּכָל־צוֹרְרָי:

My eyes are moth eaten with grief: they grow old with all of my enemies.

סוּרוּ מִמֶּנִּי כָּל־פֹּעֲלֵי אָוֶן

Depart from me all makers of sorrow.

For the LORD
Has heard the sound
Of my weeping
The LORD has heard
My cry for mercy
The LORD
Receives
My prayer

כִּי־שָׁמַע
יְהוָה
קוֹל בִּכְיִי:
שָׁמַע יְהוָה
תְּחִנָּתִי
יְהוָה
תְּפִלָּתִי יִקָּח:

All my enemies will feel shame
And be utterly dismayed
They will turn back
They will be suddenly ashamed.

יֵבֹשׁוּ וְיִבָּהֲלוּ
מְאֹד כָּל־אֹיְבָי
יָשֻׁבוּ יֵבֹשׁוּ רָגַע:

לַמְנַצֵּחַ

For the worship leader:

עַל־הַגִּתִּית

On the gittith

מִזְמוֹר לְדָוִד:

A Hymn of David

LORD our Lord
How majestic is your name
In all the earth
Whose glory
Is chanted above the heavens!
Out of the mouths of children
And suckling babies
You have founded a stronghold of praise
To answer your enemies
To silence the opponent and the avenger.

יְהוָה אֲדֹנֵינוּ
מָה־אַדִּיר שִׁמְךָ
בְּכָל־הָאָרֶץ
אֲשֶׁר תְּנָה
הוֹדְךָ עַל־הַשָּׁמָיִם:
מִפִּי עוֹלְלִים
וְיֹנְקִים
יִסַּדְתָּ עֹז
לְמַעַן צוֹרְרֶיךָ
לְהַשְׁבִּית אוֹיֵב וּמִתְנַקֵּם:

When I look at your heavens
The work of your fingers
The moon and the stars which you created,
What is man that you remember him
The son of man that you visit?
But you made him little less than God
And crown him with glory and splendour!
You make him Lord of the work of your hand
You have put all things under his feet.

כִּי־אֶרְאֶה שָׁמֶיךָ
מַעֲשֵׂי אֶצְבְּעֹתֶיךָ
יָרֵחַ וְכוֹכָבִים אֲשֶׁר כּוֹנָנְתָּה:
מָה־אֱנוֹשׁ כִּי־תִזְכְּרֶנּוּ
וּבֶן־אָדָם כִּי תִפְקְדֶנּוּ:
וַתְּחַסְּרֵהוּ מְעַט מֵאֱלֹהִים
וְכָבוֹד וְהָדָר תְּעַטְּרֵהוּ:
תַּמְשִׁילֵהוּ בְּמַעֲשֵׂי יָדֶיךָ
כֹּל שַׁתָּה תַחַת־רַגְלָיו:

Sheep and cattle, all of them
Even the beasts of the wild:
Birds of the heavens, fish of the sea,
All that passes along the path of the seas.

צֹנֶה וַאֲלָפִים כֻּלָּם
וְגַם בַּהֲמוֹת שָׂדָי:
צִפּוֹר שָׁמַיִם וּדְגֵי הַיָּם
עֹבֵר אָרְחוֹת יַמִּים:

יְהוָה אֲדֹנֵינוּ מָה־אַדִּיר

LORD our Lord how majestic

שִׁמְךָ בְּכָל־

Is your name in all

הָאָרֶץ:

The earth.

לַמְנַצֵּחַ ׀ לְעֶבֶד יְהֹוָה לְדָוִד אֲשֶׁר דִּבֶּר ׀ לַיהֹוָה אֶת־דִּבְרֵי הַשִּׁירָה
הַזֹּאת בְּיוֹם הִצִּיל־יְהֹוָה אוֹתוֹ מִכַּף כָּל־אֹיְבָיו
וּמִיַּד שָׁאוּל:

For the worship leader: of David the servant of the LORD who spoke to the LORD the words of
this song on the day that the LORD delivered him from the palms of all his enemies
and from the hand of Saul.

He said:

I love you, LORD my strength.

My mountain stronghold

And my deliverer.

My God is my rock

I take my refuge in him

My shield, my horn of salvation

My mountain stronghold.

I cry out to the LORD

Who is worthy to be praised

And I am saved from my enemies.

The cords of death

Entangled me

The floods of ruin

Fell upon me

The ropes of death

Coiled round me

The snares of death

Enmeshed me.

אֲפָפֻנִי

חֶבְלֵי־מָוֶת

וְנַחֲלֵי בְלִיַּעַל

יְבַעֲתוּנִי:

חֶבְלֵי שְׁאוֹל

סְבָבוּנִי

קִדְּמוּנִי

מוֹקְשֵׁי מָוֶת:

In my distress I called to the LORD
I cried for help to my God:

"Let him hear my voice
From his temple
Let my cry for help
Come to his ears!"

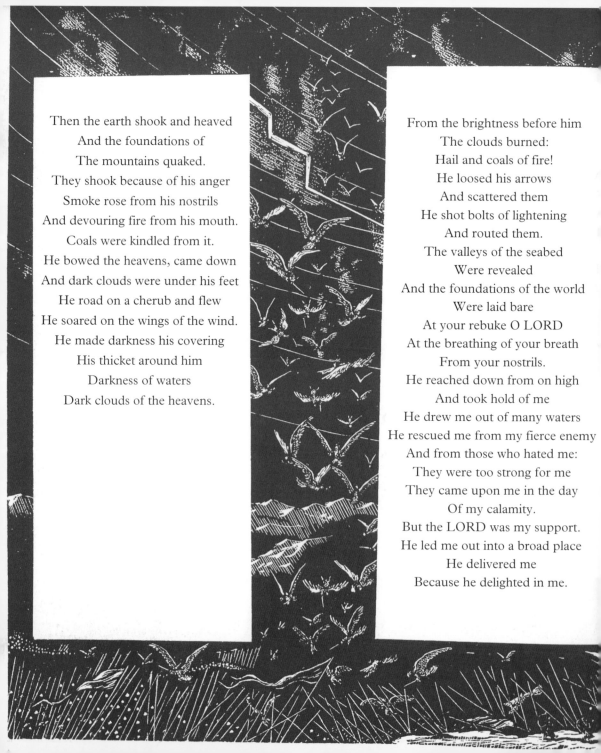

Then the earth shook and heaved
And the foundations of
The mountains quaked.
They shook because of his anger
Smoke rose from his nostrils
And devouring fire from his mouth.
Coals were kindled from it.
He bowed the heavens, came down
And dark clouds were under his feet
He road on a cherub and flew
He soared on the wings of the wind.
He made darkness his covering
His thicket around him
Darkness of waters
Dark clouds of the heavens.

From the brightness before him
The clouds burned:
Hail and coals of fire!
He loosed his arrows
And scattered them
He shot bolts of lightening
And routed them.
The valleys of the seabed
Were revealed
And the foundations of the world
Were laid bare
At your rebuke O LORD
At the breathing of your breath
From your nostrils.
He reached down from on high
And took hold of me
He drew me out of many waters
He rescued me from my fierce enemy
And from those who hated me:
They were too strong for me
They came upon me in the day
Of my calamity.
But the LORD was my support.
He led me out into a broad place
He delivered me
Because he delighted in me.

The LORD has dealt with me
According to my righteousness.
He has dealt with me
According to the purity of my hands.
For I have kept the ways of the LORD
And I have not strayed from my God.
For all his judgements are before me
And I have not cast from me
His decrees and I was pure before him
And kept myself from my sinfulness
And the LORD has dealt with me
According to my righteousness
According to the purity of my hands
In the sight of his eyes.
To the faithful you are faithful
With the man of integrity
You deal with integrity
To one who purifies himself
You show yourself pure.

But you wrestle with the perverted
For you save oppressed people
But humble proud eyes
For you light my candle
LORD my God
You shine light in my darkness
For with you I can run upon
A marauding band
And with my God
I can leap over a wall.
This God, his way is perfect!
The word of the LORD
Is tried in the fire
He is a shield for all
Who take refuge in him.
For who is a God
Apart from the LORD?
This God
Who clothes me with strength
And makes my way perfect!
He makes my feet like hinds feet
And makes me stand on high places.

He trains my hands for battle
And my arms to bend a bow of bronze
You give me the shield of your salvation
You support me with your right hand:
But your gentleness has made me great.
You will broaden my path beneath me
So my ankles will not turn.
I will pursue my enemies
And overtake them
I will not return until they are destroyed
I will strike them down so they cannot rise
They will fall under my feet.
For you have clothed me
With strength for battle
You will force those who rise against me
To their knees.
You will make my enemies
Flee before me
And I will silence those who hate me.
They will cry to the LORD but he will
Not answer them.
I will crush them like dust in the wind
I will crush them like mud of the street.
You will deliver me
From the strife of the people
You will make me ruler of the nations.
A people I have not known will serve me
When their ears hear they will obey me.
The sons of the stranger will shrink before me
The sons of the stranger will grow faint
And come trembling from their strongholds.

The LORD lives!
And blessed be my rock!
And may the God
Of my salvation
Be exalted!
This God who avenges me
Who subdues people under me
My deliver from my enemies!
Yes who raises me above those
Who rises against me,
Who rescues me from
The man of violence.
Therefore O LORD I will praise
You among the nations
And sing to your name:

He makes great victories

For his king

And shows everlasting love

To his messiah

To David and his seed

For evermore".

מִגְדִּל יְשׁוּעוֹת

מַלְכּוֹ

וְעֹשֶׂה חֶסֶד

לִמְשִׁיחוֹ

לְדָוִד וּלְזַרְעוֹ

עַד־עוֹלָם:

For the worship leader
A Hymn of David

לַמְנַצֵּחַ
מִזְמוֹר לְדָוִד:

The heavens are declaring the
The glory of God
The fields of sky are proclaiming
The work of his hands.
Day unto day pours forth speech
Night unto night
Makes known knowledge.
There is no speech, there are no words
Their voice is not heard:
Their cry goes out to all the earth
Their words to the end of the world.
In them he has pitched a tent for
The sun!
And he is like a bridegroom
Coming forth from his marriage tent
He rejoices like a strong man
To run his race
His rising is at the end of the heavens
And his circuit is toward their end
And nothing is hidden from his heat.

הַשָּׁמַיִם מְסַפְּרִים
כְּבוֹד־אֵל
וּמַעֲשֵׂה יָדָיו
מַגִּיד הָרָקִיעַ:
יוֹם לְיוֹם יַבִּיעַ אֹמֶר
וְלַיְלָה לְּלַיְלָה
יְחַוֶּה־דָּעַת:
אֵין־אֹמֶר וְאֵין דְּבָרִים
בְּלִי נִשְׁמָע קוֹלָם:
בְּכָל־הָאָרֶץ ׀ יָצָא קַוָּם
בִּקְצֵה תֵבֵל מִלֵּיהֶם
לַשֶּׁמֶשׁ
שָׂם־אֹהֶל בָּהֶם:
וְהוּא כְּחָתָן
יֹצֵא מֵחֻפָּתוֹ
יָשִׂישׂ כְּגִבּוֹר
לָרוּץ אֹרַח:
מִקְצֵה הַשָּׁמַיִם ׀ מוֹצָאוֹ
וּתְקוּפָתוֹ עַל־קְצוֹתָם
וְאֵין נִסְתָּר מֵחַמָּתוֹ:

The law of the LORD is perfect
Restoring the soul
The testimony of the LORD is trustworthy
Making wise the simple
The precepts of the LORD are right
Giving joy to the heart
The commandment of the LORD is clear
Giving light to the eyes
The fear of the LORD is clean
Enduring forever
The judgements of the LORD are truth
They are altogether righteous.
More to be desired than gold
Than much fine gold
Sweeter than honey and honey
From the honeycomb.
And your servant is instructed by them
And in keeping them there is great reward.

Who is aware of unintentional sins?
Cleanse me from hidden faults!
Hold back your servant from defiant sins
Let them not rule me!
Then I will be whole
And cleansed from great sin.
May the words of my mouth
And the thoughts of my heart
Be acceptable in your presence
O LORD my rock and my redeemer.

      On help at day break. A Hymn of David

כב לַמְנַצֵּחַ
עַל־אַיֶּלֶת הַשַּׁחַר מִזְמוֹר לְדָוִד׃

אֵלִי אֵלִי לָמָה עֲזַבְתָּנִי

My God, my God, why have you forsaken me?
Why so distant from my rescue and the sound of my shrieking?

רָחוֹק מִישׁוּעָתִי דִּבְרֵי שַׁאֲגָתִי׃

My God I cry out by day   אֱלֹהַי אֶקְרָא יוֹמָם
But you do not answer   וְלֹא תַעֲנֶה
I cry out by night   וְלַיְלָה
But for me there is no rest.   וְלֹא־דוּמִיָּה לִי׃

But you are holy   וְאַתָּה קָדוֹשׁ
You are enthroned on the praises of Israel.   יוֹשֵׁב תְּהִלּוֹת יִשְׂרָאֵל׃
Our fathers trusted in you   בְּךָ בָּטְחוּ אֲבֹתֵינוּ
They trusted in you and you delivered them   בָּטְחוּ וַתְּפַלְּטֵמוֹ׃
They cried to you and were delivered   אֵלֶיךָ זָעֲקוּ וְנִמְלָטוּ
They trusted and were not ashamed.   בְּךָ בָטְחוּ וְלֹא־בוֹשׁוּ׃
But I am a worm and no man   וְאָנֹכִי תוֹלַעַת וְלֹא־אִישׁ
An offence to mankind   חֶרְפַּת אָדָם
And despised by the people!   וּבְזוּי עָם׃
All who see me deride   כָּל־רֹאַי יַלְעִגוּ לִי
They curl their lip and shake their head   יַפְטִירוּ בְשָׂפָה יָנִיעוּ רֹאשׁ׃
"He threw himself on the LORD   גֹּל אֶל־יְהוָה

Let the LORD rescue   יְפַלְּטֵהוּ
Let him deliver him   יַצִּילֵהוּ
If he delights in him!"   כִּי חָפֵץ בּוֹ׃
But you drew me from the womb   כִּי־אַתָּה גֹחִי מִבָּטֶן
Laying me on the breasts of my mother   מַבְטִיחִי עַל־שְׁדֵי אִמִּי׃
I was laid upon you from the womb.   עָלֶיךָ הָשְׁלַכְתִּי מֵרָחֶם
You are my God   מִבֶּטֶן אִמִּי
From the womb of my mother.   אֵלִי אָתָּה׃

Do not be distant from me   אַל־תִּרְחַק מִמֶּנִּי
For trouble is near, there is no one to help.   כִּי־צָרָה קְרוֹבָה כִּי־אֵין עוֹזֵר׃
Many young bulls have surrounded me   סְבָבוּנִי פָּרִים רַבִּים
Mighty bulls of Bashan have encircled me   אַבִּירֵי בָשָׁן כִּתְּרוּנִי׃
A rending roaring lion!   פָּצוּ עָלַי פִּיהֶם
Against me they open wide their jaws.   אַרְיֵה טֹרֵף וְשֹׁאֵג׃
I am poured out like water: כַּמַּיִם נִשְׁפַּכְתִּי
All my bones have fallen apart   וְהִתְפָּרְדוּ כָּל־עַצְמוֹתָי
My heart has become like wax: it has melted inside me.   הָיָה לִבִּי כַּדּוֹנָג נָמֵס בְּתוֹךְ מֵעָי׃
My strength like baked clay has dried up,   יָבֵשׁ כַּחֶרֶשׂ כֹּחִי
My tongue has been made to stick to my mouth.   וּלְשׁוֹנִי מֻדְבָּק מַלְקוֹחָי
You are laying me in the dust of death   וְלַעֲפַר־מָוֶת תִּשְׁפְּתֵנִי׃
 For dogs have surrounded me,   כִּי סְבָבוּנִי כְּלָבִים
An assembly of the wicked have surrounded me.   עֲדַת מְרֵעִים הִקִּיפוּנִי
They have pierced my hands and my feet.   כָּאֲרִי יָדַי וְרַגְלָי׃

I can count exactly all my bones   אֲסַפֵּר כָּל־עַצְמוֹתָי
But they gloat and stare at me   הֵמָּה יַבִּיטוּ יִרְאוּ־בִי׃
They divide my clothes among them   יְחַלְּקוּ בְגָדַי לָהֶם
And for my robes they cast lots.   וְעַל־לְבוּשִׁי יַפִּילוּ גוֹרָל׃

But you LORD do not be distant   וְאַתָּה יְהוָה אַל־תִּרְחָק
My help hurry to help me   אֱיָלוּתִי לְעֶזְרָתִי חוּשָׁה׃
From the sword deliver my life   הַצִּילָה מֵחֶרֶב נַפְשִׁי
From the power of the dog deliver my only possession   מִיַּד־כֶּלֶב יְחִידָתִי׃
Save me from the mouth of the lion   הוֹשִׁיעֵנִי מִפִּי אַרְיֵה
From the horns of the wild ox   וּמִקַּרְנֵי רֵמִים

You have answered me!   עֲנִיתָנִי׃

I will make your name known
To my brothers!
In the middle of your congregation
I will praise you:

"You who fear the LORD
Praise him!
Let all the seed of Jacob
Honour him
And all the seed of Israel
Stand in awe before him.

אַסַפְּרָה שִׁמְךָ
לְאֶחָי
בְּתוֹךְ קָהָל
אֲהַלְלֶךָ:

יִרְאֵי יְהוָה
הַלְלוּהוּ
כָּל־זֶרַע יַעֲקֹב
כַּבְּדוּהוּ
וְגוּרוּ מִמֶּנּוּ
כָּל־זֶרַע יִשְׂרָאֵל:

For he does not despise
He does not disdain
The suffering of the afflicted
He did not hide his face from him
He cried to him
And he heard".

כִּי לֹא־בָזָה
וְלֹא שִׁקַּץ
עֱנוּת עָנִי
וְלֹא־הִסְתִּיר פָּנָיו מִמֶּנּוּ
וּבְשַׁוְּעוֹ אֵלָיו
שָׁמֵעַ:

My praising in the great assembly
Comes from you:
I will fulfil my promises
Before those who fear him
Let the poor eat and be satisfied!
Let those who seek him
Praise the LORD!
May your hearts live for ever!
All the ends of the earth
Will remember
And return to the LORD
And all the families of nations
Will bow down before you
For the kingdom is the LORD's
He rules the nations.

מֵאִתְּךָ תְהִלָּתִי
בְּקָהָל רָב
נְדָרַי אֲשַׁלֵּם
נֶגֶד יְרֵאָיו:
יֹאכְלוּ עֲנָוִים וְיִשְׂבָּעוּ
יְהַלְלוּ יְהוָה
דֹּרְשָׁיו
יְחִי לְבַבְכֶם לָעַד:
יִזְכְּרוּ וְיָשֻׁבוּ
אֶל־יְהוָה
כָּל־אַפְסֵי־אָרֶץ
וְיִשְׁתַּחֲווּ לְפָנֶיךָ
כָּל־מִשְׁפְּחוֹת גּוֹיִם:
כִּי לַיהוָה הַמְּלוּכָה
וּמֹשֵׁל בַּגּוֹיִם:

All the fat ones of the earth eat and bow down:
Before him will bow down
All who go down to the dust
Each one who cannot preserve his own life.

אָכְלוּ וַיִּשְׁתַּחֲווּ כָּל־דִּשְׁנֵי־אֶרֶץ
לְפָנָיו יִכְרְעוּ
יֹרְדֵי עָפָר כָּל־
וְנַפְשׁוֹ לֹא חִיָּה:

A seed
Will serve him
The Lord
Will be made known
To a generation
That will come.
His deliverance
Will be made known
To a people
That will be born:

זֶרַע
יַעַבְדֶנּוּ
יְסֻפַּר
לַאדֹנָי
לַדּוֹר:

יָבֹאוּ וְיַגִּידוּ
צִדְקָתוֹ
לְעַם
נוֹלָד:

He has done it! כִּי עָשָׂה:

A Hymn of David

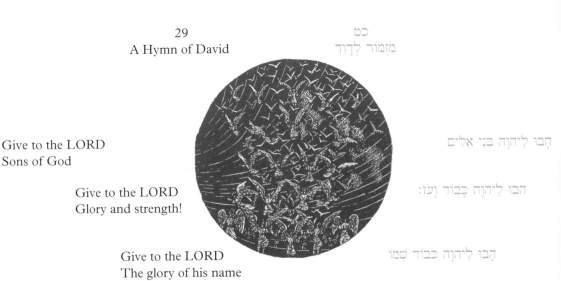

כט
מִזְמוֹר לְדָוִד

Give to the LORD
Sons of God

הָבוּ לַיהוָה בְּנֵי אֵלִים

Give to the LORD
Glory and strength!

הָבוּ לַיהוָה כָּבוֹד וָעֹז:

Give to the LORD
The glory of his name

הָבוּ לַיהוָה כְּבוֹד שְׁמוֹ

Bow down to the LORD
In the glory of holiness

הִשְׁתַּחֲווּ לַיהוָה
בְּהַדְרַת־קֹדֶשׁ:

The voice of the LORD
Is over the waters
The God of glory thunders
The LORD is over
The mighty waters

קוֹל יְהוָה
עַל־הַמָּיִם
אֵל־הַכָּבוֹד הִרְעִים
יְהוָה עַל־
מַיִם רַבִּים:

The voice of the LORD
Is full of power
The voice of the LORD
Is full of majesty

קוֹל־יְהוָה בַּכֹּחַ
קוֹל יְהוָה בֶּהָדָר:

The voice of the LORD
Breaks the cedars
The LORD breaks
The cedars of Lebanon

קוֹל יְהוָה שֹׁבֵר אֲרָזִים
וַיְשַׁבֵּר יְהוָה
אֶת־אַרְזֵי הַלְּבָנוֹן:

He makes Lebanon
Skip like a calf
Sirion like a young wild ox

וַיַּרְקִידֵם כְּמוֹ־עֵגֶל לְבָנוֹן
וְשִׂרְיֹן כְּמוֹ בֶן־רְאֵמִים:

The voice of the LORD
Forks the flames of fire

    The voice of the LORD
    Makes the wilderness
    Tremble
    The LORD makes
    The wilderness of Kadesh
    Tremble.
        The voice of the LORD
        Makes the oaks writhe
        And strips the forests

                And in his temple
                    All cries
                      "Glory!"

                    The LORD sat
          Enthroned at the flood
                  The LORD sits
    Enthroned as king forever.

The LORD
Will give strength
To his people

The LORD
Will bless
His people
With peace.

קוֹל־יְהוָה
חֹצֵב לַהֲבוֹת אֵשׁ:

קוֹל יְהוָה
יָחִיל מִדְבָּר

יָחִיל יְהוָה מִדְבַּר קָדֵשׁ:

קוֹל יְהוָה ׀
יְחוֹלֵל אַיָּלוֹת
וַיֶּחֱשֹׂף־יְעָרוֹת

וּבְהֵיכָלוֹ
כֻּלּוֹ אֹמֵר
כָּבוֹד:

יְהוָה
לַמַּבּוּל יָשָׁב
וַיֵּשֶׁב יְהוָה
מֶלֶךְ לְעוֹלָם:

יְהוָה
עֹז לְעַמּוֹ
יִתֵּן

יְהוָה ׀
יְבָרֵךְ
אֶת־עַמּוֹ
בַשָּׁלוֹם:

A Hymn, a song at the dedication of the House.
Of David

מִזְמוֹר שִׁיר־חֲנֻכַּת הַבַּיִת
לְדָוִד:

I will exalt you O LORD
For you have drawn me up
You have not made my enemies exult over me.
LORD my God
I cried to you for help
And you healed me
LORD you brought my soul up from the grave
From among those going down to the pit
You gave me life.
Make music to the LORD his loved ones
And give thanks to his holy name!

אֲרוֹמִמְךָ יְהוָה
כִּי דִלִּיתָנִי
וְלֹא־שִׂמַּחְתָּ אֹיְבַי לִי:
יְהוָה אֱלֹהָי
שִׁוַּעְתִּי אֵלֶיךָ
וַתִּרְפָּאֵנִי:
יְהוָה הֶעֱלִיתָ מִן־שְׁאוֹל נַפְשִׁי
חִיִּיתַנִי
מִיָּרְדִי־בוֹר:
זַמְּרוּ לַיהוָה חֲסִידָיו
וְהוֹדוּ לְזֵכֶר קָדְשׁוֹ:

For his anger
Is for a moment
His acceptance
Is life!
At evening
Weeping comes to stay
But in the morning
Is joy!

כִּי רֶגַע בְּאַפּוֹ
חַיִּים בִּרְצוֹנוֹ
בָּעֶרֶב יָלִין
בֶּכִי וְלַבֹּקֶר
רִנָּה:

But I, in my prosperity I said
"I will never be shaken"
LORD you established my mountain stronghold
In your grace:
When you hid your face
I became frightened.
I will cry out to you LORD
I will plead to my lord.
What gain is there in my blood
When I go down to the pit?
Will it declare your truth?
Hear LORD and be gracious to me
LORD be my help.

וַאֲנִי אָמַרְתִּי בְשַׁלְוִי:
בַּל־אֶמּוֹט לְעוֹלָם:
יְהוָה בִּרְצוֹנְךָ הֶעֱמַדְתָּה לְהַרְרִי עֹז
הִסְתַּרְתָּ פָנֶיךָ
הָיִיתִי נִבְהָל:
אֵלֶיךָ יְהוָה אֶקְרָא
וְאֶל־אֲדֹנָי אֶתְחַנָּן:
מַה־בֶּצַע בְּדָמִי
בְּרִדְתִּי אֶל־שָׁחַת
הֲיוֹדְךָ עָפָר הֲיַגִּיד אֲמִתֶּךָ:
שְׁמַע־יְהוָה וְחָנֵּנִי
יְהוָה הֱיֵה־עֹזֵר לִי:

You turned my mourning
Into dancing!
You untied my sackcloth
And clothed me with joy!

הָפַכְתָּ מִסְפְּדִי
לְמָחוֹל לִי
פִּתַּחְתָּ שַׂקִּי
וַתְּאַזְּרֵנִי שִׂמְחָה:

So that my spirit will make music to you
And not be silent
LORD my God I will give thanks to you forever.

לְמַעַן יְזַמֶּרְךָ כָבוֹד
וְלֹא יִדֹּם
יְהוָה אֱלֹהַי לְעוֹלָם אוֹדֶךָּ:

38 A Hymn of David. To remind.

לֹח מִזְמוֹר לְדָוִד לְהַזְכִּיר:

יְהוָה אַל־בְּקֶצְפְּךָ תוֹכִיחֵנִי וּבַחֲמָתְךָ תְיַסְּרֵנִי:

LORD do not in your rage punish me or in your anger discipline me

כִּי־חִצֶּיךָ נִחֲתוּ בִי וַתִּנְחַת עָלַי יָדֶךָ:

For your arrows have sunk into me and your hand has come down upon me.
Because of your indignation there is no soundness in my flesh,
Because of my sin there is no peace in my bones.

אֵין־מְתֹם בִּבְשָׂרִי מִפְּנֵי

זַעְמֶךָ אֵין־שָׁלוֹם בַּעֲצָמַי מִפְּנֵי חַטָּאתִי:

כִּי עֲוֹנֹתַי עָבְרוּ רֹאשִׁי כְּמַשָּׂא כָבֵד יִכְבְּדוּ מִמֶּנִּי:

For my foolish deeds have broken over my head, like a heavy burden they are too heavy for me.
Because of my foolishness my stripes stink and putrify.

הִבְאִישׁוּ נָמַקּוּ חַבּוּרֹתָי מִפְּנֵי אִוַּלְתִּי:

נַעֲוֵיתִי שַׁחֹתִי עַד־מְאֹד כָּל־הַיּוֹם קֹדֵר הִלָּכְתִּי:

I am bowed down, completely broken down, all day long I go about dirty.
For my loins are full of burning, there is no soundness in my flesh.
I grow cold. I am completely crushed.
I grown from the groaning of my heart.

כִּי־כְסָלַי מָלְאוּ נִקְלֶה וְאֵין מְתֹם בִּבְשָׂרִי:

נְפוּגוֹתִי וְנִדְכֵּיתִי עַד־מְאֹד

שָׁאַגְתִּי מִנַּהֲמַת לִבִּי:

Lord
All my longings
Are before you
My sighings
Are not hidden
From you.

אֲדֹנָי נֶגְדְּךָ

כָל־תַּאֲוָתִי וְאַנְחָתִי

מִמְּךָ לֹא־נִסְתָּרָה:

לִבִּי סְחַרְחַר עֲזָבַנִי כֹחִי וְאוֹר־עֵינַי גַּם־הֵם אֵין אִתִּי:

My heart throbs my strength leaves me; even the light of my eyes goes from me.

אֹהֲבַי וְרֵעַי מִנֶּגֶד נִגְעִי יַעֲמֹדוּ וּקְרוֹבַי מֵרָחֹק עָמָדוּ:

My loved ones and friends stay aloof from my plague, my relatives stay at a distance.
Those that seek my life set traps,
Those that speak my harm speak of "pits of destruction"
All day long they mutter lies.
But I am like a deaf man, I do not hear.
I am like a dumb man that does not open his mouth.
I have become like a man who does not hear and in whose mouth are no arguments.
Because I wait for you LORD, you will answer Lord my God

וַיְנַקְשׁוּ מְבַקְשֵׁי נַפְשִׁי וְדֹרְשֵׁי רָעָתִי

דִּבְּרוּ הַוּוֹת וּמִרְמוֹת כָּל־הַיּוֹם יֶהְגּוּ:

וַאֲנִי כְחֵרֵשׁ לֹא אֶשְׁמָע וּכְאִלֵּם לֹא יִפְתַּח־פִּיו:

וָאֱהִי כְּאִישׁ אֲשֶׁר לֹא־שֹׁמֵעַ וְאֵין בְּפִיו תּוֹכָחוֹת:

כִּי־לְךָ יְהוָה הוֹחָלְתִּי אַתָּה תַעֲנֶה אֲדֹנָי אֱלֹהָי:

For I said: "in case they gloat over me, or exult themselves over me when my foot stumbles.
For I am ready to fall, my pain is with me continually.
I will confess my evil, I am anxious about my sin
My enemies without cause are dangerous,
Those who hate me through falsehoods have become many.
And those who return evil for good
Act as enemies because I pursue good.

כִּי־אָמַרְתִּי פֶּן־יִשְׂמְחוּ־לִי בְּמוֹט רַגְלִי עָלַי הִגְדִּילוּ:

כִּי־אֲנִי לְצֶלַע נָכוֹן וּמַכְאוֹבִי נֶגְדִּי תָמִיד:

כִּי־עֲוֹנִי אַגִּיד אֶדְאַג מֵחַטָּאתִי:

וְאֹיְבַי חַיִּים עָצֵמוּ

רַבּוּ שֹׂנְאַי שָׁקֶר:

וּמְשַׁלְּמֵי רָעָה תַּחַת טוֹבָה

יִשְׂטְנוּנִי תַּחַת רָדֳפִי־טוֹב:

LORD do not forsake me!
My God do not be far from me !
Be quick to help me
Lord of my salvation.

אַל־תַּעַזְבֵנִי יְהוָה

אֱלֹהַי אַל־תִּרְחַק מִמֶּנִּי:

חוּשָׁה לְעֶזְרָתִי

אֲדֹנָי תְּשׁוּעָתִי:

42   For the worship leader a maskil of the Sons of Korah מב לַמְנַצֵּחַ מַשְׂכִּיל לִבְנֵי־קֹרַח:

As a hind yearns כְּאַיָּל תַּעֲרֹג

For rivers of water עַל־אֲפִיקֵי־מָיִם

So my soul כֵּן נַפְשִׁי

Yearns for you תַעֲרֹג אֵלֶיךָ

Oh God אֱלֹהִים:

My soul is thirsty for God
For the living God
When shall I come and appear
Before the presence of God ?
My tears have been my bread
Day and night
When all day he says to me
"Where is your God?"
These things will I remember,
(And pour out my innermost being)
That I will process with the throng
I would lead the procession to the house of God
With shouts of joy and thanksgiving
A noise of pilgrimage

Why are you oppressed מַה־תִּשְׁתּוֹחֲחִי
My soul נַפְשִׁי
Why do you groan וַתֶּהֱמִי
Within me? עָלָי
Hope in God הוֹחִילִי לֵאלֹהִים
For I will still praise him כִּי־עוֹד אוֹדֶנּוּ
My salvation יְשׁוּעֹת פָּנָי
And my God וֵאלֹהָי:

O my God אֱלֹהַי
My soul is very עָלַי נַפְשִׁי
Oppressed תִשְׁתּוֹחָח
Therefore I remember you עַל־כֵּן אֶזְכָּרְךָ
From the land of Jordan מֵאֶרֶץ יַרְדֵּן
And the range of Hermon וְחֶרְמוֹנִים
From mountain of Mijar מֵהַר מִצְעָר:
Deep calls unto Deep תְּהוֹם־אֶל־תְּהוֹם קוֹרֵא
In the roar of your cataracts לְקוֹל צִנּוֹרֶיךָ
All your breakers כָּל־מִשְׁבָּרֶיךָ
And your waves וְגַלֶּיךָ
Have passed over me עָלַי עָבָרוּ:

By day the Lord ordains his love for me
By night his song is with me
A prayer to the God of my life
I will say unto God my rock
"Why have you forgotten me?"
"Why do I walk in darkness
In the oppressions of an enemy?"
Breaking my bones my opponents taunt me,
All day long they say to me
"Where is your God?"

Why are you oppressed
My soul
Why do you groan
Within me?
Hope in God
For I will still praise him
My salvation
And my God

43

מה תשתוחחי ׀
נפשי
ותהמי
עלי
הוחילי לאלהים
כי־עוד אודנו
ישועת פני
ואלהי׃

מג

Vindicate me God plead my case
Against a nation who have not love
Rescue me from deceitful and unjust men.
For you are the God of my refuge
"Why have you rejected me?
Why do I walk around in darkness
In the oppression of an enemy?"
Send your light and your truth
Let them lead me
Let them bring me to your holy mountain
And to the places where you dwell
I will go to the altar of God
To God the joy of my rejoicing
I will praise you on the kinnor
O God my God

Why are you oppressed
My soul
Why do you groan
Within me?
Hope in God
For I will still praise him
My salvation
And my God.

מה תשתוחחי ׀
נפשי
ותהמי
עלי
הוחילי לאלהים
כי־עוד אודנו
ישועת פני
ואלהי׃

For the worship leader
of the sons of Korah a maskil

לַמְנַצֵּחַ
לִבְנֵי־קֹרַח מַשְׂכִּיל:

We have heard with our ears O God
Our fathers have told us
Of the deeds you did in their days
In the days of old
You by your hand did dispossess the nations
And planted them.
You afflicted the peoples and let them grow.
For it was not by their sword they possessed the land
It was not their arm that saved them.
It was your right hand and your arm
And the light of your face:
For you loved them.
You are my king O God
Ordaining victories for Israel !
Through you we throw down our opponents
In your name we trample down
Those who rise against us.
For I will not trust my bow
My sword will not save me
For you have saved us from our opponents
And shamed those who hate us
We have gloried in God all day long
And will praise your name for ever.

Selah: סֶלָה

And then you reject us and humiliate us
You do not go about with our armies
You make us retreat from the enemy
And those who hate us despoil us for themselves.
You give us for food, like sheep
You scatter us in the nations
You sell your people for nothing
You gain nothing by their sale
You make us a joke to our neighbours
An object of scorn and derision
To those who surround us.
You make us a proverb in the nations
A cause for head shaking among the peoples.
My shame is in front of me all day
And my face is covered with shame
Because of a mocking and blasphemous voice
The presence of an enemy and an avenger

All this has come upon us
Though we have not forgotten you
We have not been false to your covenant
Our heart has not slid back
Our step has not turned back from your path.
But you have reduced us to a haunt of jackals
And spread over us a shadow of death
If we had forgotten the name of our God
And spread out our palms to a strange God
Would not God have found this out
For he knows the secrets of the heart.

But no, it is for your sake
We are killed
All the day long
We are reckoned
As sheep for the slaughter

כִּי־עָלֶיךָ
הֹרַגְנוּ
כָל־הַיּוֹם
נֶחְשַׁבְנוּ
כְּצֹאן טִבְחָה:

Wake up!

Why

Do you sleep

Lord?

Wake up!

Do not

Reject us

For ever!

עוּרָה ׀

לָמָּה

תִישַׁן ׀

אֲדֹנָי

הָקִיצָה

אַל־

תִּזְנַח

לָנֶצַח:

Why do you hide your face
And forget our affliction
And our oppression
For our soul sinks into the dust
Our body is joined to the earth

Rise up! Help us!
Redeem us because of your love.

For the Worship Leader
Of the Sons of Korah
On Soprano. A Song

לַמְנַצֵּחַ
לִבְנֵי־קֹרַח
עַל־עֲלָמוֹת שִׁיר:

מו

God is our refuge and strength
A very present help in trouble
Therefore we will not fear
Though the earth quakes
And the mountains slide
Into the heart of the sea.
And the mountains quake
At its swelling

Selah :סֶלָה

There is a river
Whose streams make glad
The city of God
The holy dwelling place
Of the Most High
God is in the midst of her:
She will not fall.
God will help her
At break of day.
Nations roar
Kingdoms slide
He raises his voice:
The earth dissolves.
The LORD of Hosts is with us
The God of Jacob is our high refuge

נָהָר
פְּלָגָיו יְשַׂמְּחוּ
עִיר־אֱלֹהִים
קְדֹשׁ מִשְׁכְּנֵי
עֶלְיוֹן:
אֱלֹהִים בְּקִרְבָּהּ
בַּל־תִּמּוֹט
יַעְזְרֶהָ אֱלֹהִים
לִפְנוֹת בֹּקֶר:
הָמוּ גוֹיִם
מָטוּ מַמְלָכוֹת
נָתַן בְּקוֹלוֹ
תָּמוּג אָרֶץ:
יְהוָה צְבָאוֹת עִמָּנוּ
מִשְׂגָּב־לָנוּ אֱלֹהֵי יַעֲקֹב

Selah :סֶלָה

Come and see the works of the LORD
What desolations
He has brought upon the earth.
To the ends of the earth
He makes wars cease.
He breaks a bow
He snaps a spear in two
He burns shields in the fire.
Be still!
Know that I am God
I will be exalted
Among the nations
I will be exalted
In the earth.
The LORD of Hosts is with us
The God of Jacob is our high refuge.

Selah :סֶלָה

A song. A Hymn of the sons of Korah שִׁיר מִזְמוֹר לִבְנֵי־קֹרַח: מח

Great is the LORD greatly to be praised
In the city of our God is his holy mountain
Beautiful in its height
The exultation of the whole earth
Mount Sion
The utter north
The city of the great king.
God is in her citadels
He has made himself known as her high refuge
For see: the kings gathered, they advanced together
They saw, they were astounded, they praised, they fled
There they were seized with trembling
Writhing as with childbirth
Like an east wind shatters the ships of Tarshish
As we have heard so we have seen
In the city of the Lord of Hosts In the city of our God
That God has secured it forever

Selah סֶלָה:

We have imagined
Your love O God
In the midst of
Your temple
O God as is your name
So is your praise
To the ends of the earth
Your right hand
Is full of righteousness
Mount Sion will be glad
The daughters of Judah
Rejoice
Because of
Your judgements
Go round Sion
Make a circuit
Of her
Count her towers

דִּמִּינוּ
אֱלֹהִים חַסְדֶּךָ
בְּקֶרֶב
הֵיכָלֶךָ:
כְּשִׁמְךָ אֱלֹהִים
כֵּן תְּהִלָּתְךָ
עַל־קַצְוֵי־אֶרֶץ
צֶדֶק
מָלְאָה יְמִינֶךָ:
יִשְׂמַח הַר־צִיּוֹן
תָּגֵלְנָה
בְּנוֹת יְהוּדָה
לְמַעַן
מִשְׁפָּטֶיךָ:
סֹבּוּ צִיּוֹן
הַקִּיפוּהָ
סִפְרוּ
מִגְדָּלֶיהָ:

Put her defences in your heart
Consider her citadels
That you may recount it to another generation

שִׁיתוּ לִבְּכֶם ׀ לְחֵילָה
פַּסְּגוּ אַרְמְנוֹתֶיהָ
לְמַעַן תְּסַפְּרוּ לְדוֹר אַחֲרוֹן:

For this God
Is our God
For ever and ever
He will be our guide
Even unto death.

49 For the worship leader
A Hymn of the sons of Korah

מ֫ לַמְנַצֵּ֥חַ ׀
לִבְנֵי־קֹ֬רַח מִזְמֽוֹר׃

Hear this all peoples! Listen all who dwell in the passing world
Both sons of Adam and sons of distinguished men,
Rich and poor together
My mouth shall speak wisdoms the meditations of my heart
Are understandings
I will tune my ear to a proverb, I will solve my riddle on a harp:
Why should I fear in the days of evil
When the evil at my heels is all around me
Of those who trust in their wealth and glory in their great riches,
Truly a man is not able to redeem himself or pay to God
His own ransom
To live forever and not see the pit.
The ransom for their sons is too costly: they will cease forever
For one sees that wise men die, the stupid and the brutal
Together perish
And abandon their wealth to others
Their graves will be their everlasting houses
Their dwelling place from generation to generation
Who called their lands after their own names
Man does not lodge in splendour
He is destroyed like the animals
This is the path of the self confident fools and those who follow them
Who accept their mouthings

Selah סֶֽלָה׃

Like sheep they are destined for death: death is their shepherd
When morning comes honest men are their masters
Their forms decay in death: they have no homes.

But God
Will redeem my life
From the hand
Of death
For he will
Receive me

אַ֥ךְ־אֱלֹהִ֗ים
יִפְדֶּ֣ה נַ֭פְשִׁי
מִיַּד־
שְׁא֑וֹל
כִּ֖י
יִקָּחֵ֣נִי

Do not fear when a man grows rich
When the glory of his house grows great
For when he dies he can take nothing
His glory will not go down after him
For in his life he blessed himself
(Do well for yourself and they will praise you)
But he will go to the generation of his fathers
They will never again see the light
Man in splendour without understanding
Is destroyed like the animals.

נ מִזְמוֹר לְאָסָף

אֵל ׀ אֱלֹהִים יְהוָה
דִּבֶּר וַיִּקְרָא־אָרֶץ
מִמִּזְרַח־שֶׁמֶשׁ
עַד־מְבֹאוֹ׃
מִצִּיּוֹן מִכְלַל־יֹפִי
אֱלֹהִים הוֹפִיעַ׃
יָבֹא אֱלֹהֵינוּ וְאַל־יֶחֱרַשׁ
אֵשׁ־לְפָנָיו תֹּאכֵל
וּסְבִיבָיו נִשְׂעֲרָה מְאֹד׃
יִקְרָא אֶל־הַשָּׁמַיִם מֵעָל
וְאֶל־הָאָרֶץ
לָדִין עַמּוֹ׃
אִסְפוּ־לִי חֲסִידָי
כֹּרְתֵי בְרִיתִי
עֲלֵי־זָבַח׃
וַיַּגִּידוּ שָׁמַיִם צִדְקוֹ
כִּי־אֱלֹהִים ׀ שֹׁפֵט הוּא
סֶלָה׃

god, God the LORD
Speaks and summons the earth
From the place of the sun's rising
To the place of its going down.
Out of Sion, the completion of beauty
God shines
Our God comes and will not keep silent.
Before him is consuming fire
Storm winds whirl around him.
He calls unto the heavens above
And unto the earth
To judge his people:
"Gather to me my beloved ones
Who have made a covenant with me
Of sacrifice."
The heavens declare his righteousness
For God himself is judge
　　Selah

Hear my people and I will speak:
Israel, I will protest against you
I am God, your God.
I do not chide you for your sacrifices
Your burning sacrifices
Are constantly before me.
I receive no young bulls
From your household
No he goats from your pens
For all the living creatures
Of the forest are mine
And the cattle on a thousand hills.
I know all the birds of the mountains
And the creeping things of the field
Are in my care.
If I were hungry I would not tell you
For the world and its produce are mine.
Do I eat the flesh of bulls
Or drink the blood of goats?
Make a sacrifice of thanksgiving to God
Make good your vows to the Most High.
Call on me in the day of trouble
I will rescue you and you will glory in me.

But to the wicked God says:
'What business have you to recite my laws
And to take my covenant in your mouth
You who hate discipline
Who hurl my words behind you
When you see a thief
You are well pleased with him
Your chosen life is with adulterers.
You let loose your mouth for evil
Your tongue designs deceit
You sit speaking against your brother
You malign your own mother's son
These things you did and I kept silent
You really thought
I AM like you
I will correct you and set out the charge
In front of your eyes
I beg you to consider
You who forget God
Less I tear you up
And there is no one left to save you.

He who offers a sacrifice of thanksgiving glories in me
And prepares a way where I will show him
The salvation of God.

For the worship leader, a Hymn of David
When Nathan the prophet came to him
After he had slept with Bathsheba

לַמְנַצֵּחַ מִזְמוֹר לְדָוִד:
בְּבוֹא־אֵלָיו נָתָן הַנָּבִיא
כַּאֲשֶׁר־בָּא אֶל בַּת־שָׁבַע:

Be gracious to me O God because of your love

חָנֵּנִי אֱלֹהִים כְּחַסְדֶּךָ

Because of your great compassion wipe away my rebellion.

כְּרֹב רַחֲמֶיךָ מְחֵה פְשָׁעָי:

Wash out my guilt and purify me from my sin.

הֶרֶב [הַרְבֵּה] כַּבְּסֵנִי מֵעֲוֹנִי וּמֵחַטָּאתִי טַהֲרֵנִי:

For I know my rebellions and my sin confronts me continually.

כִּי־פְשָׁעַי אֲנִי אֵדָע וְחַטָּאתִי נֶגְדִּי תָמִיד:

Against you, you alone, I have sinned and done what is evil in your eyes

לְךָ לְבַדְּךָ חָטָאתִי וְהָרַע בְּעֵינֶיךָ עָשִׂיתִי

So that you are just when you speak, justified when you pass judgement.

לְמַעַן תִּצְדַּק בְּדָבְרֶךָ תִּזְכֶּה בְשָׁפְטֶךָ:

I was born in evil, my mother conceived me in sin

הֵן־בְּעָווֹן חוֹלָלְתִּי וּבְחֵטְא יֶחֱמַתְנִי אִמִּי:

But you desire truth in the innermost being;

הֵן־אֱמֶת חָפַצְתָּ בַטֻּחוֹת

You will make me know wisdom in my secret heart

וּבְסָתֻם חָכְמָה תוֹדִיעֵנִי:

You will cleanse my sin with hyssop and I will be clean

תְּחַטְּאֵנִי בְאֵזוֹב וְאֶטְהָר

You will

Wash me

And I will be

Whiter

Than snow

תְּכַבְּסֵנִי

וּמִשֶּׁלֶג

אַלְבִּין:

You will make me hear joy and laughing
The bones you have broken will dance.

Hide your face from my sins
And wipe out all my guilt

Make a clean heart

In me O God

And make new

Within me

A firm spirit

לֵב טָהוֹר בְּרָא־

לִי אֱלֹהִים

וְרוּחַ נָכוֹן

חַדֵּשׁ

בְּקִרְבִּי :

אַל־תַּשְׁלִיכֵנִי מִלְּפָנֶיךָ וְרוּחַ קָדְשְׁךָ אַל־תִּקַּח מִמֶּנִּי :
Do not cast me from your presence, do not take from me your holy spirit

Bring back to me the joy of your deliverance
And let a willing spirit keep me firm
May I teach the rebellious your ways
And sinners will return to you

הַצִּילֵנִי מִדָּמִים ׀ אֱלֹהִים אֱלֹהֵי תְּשׁוּעָתִי
Save me from bloodguilt O God, God of my salvation.
And my tongue will sing aloud your righteousness

O Lord you will open my lips
And my mouth will proclaim your praise
You have no delight in a sacrifice or I would bring one
You will not accept a burning sacrifice
The sacrifices of God are a broken spirit
A broken spirit and a crushed heart O God
You will not despise
Be good to Sion in your favour
Rebuild the walls of Jerusalem
Then you will delight in sacrifices of righteousness
Burning sacrifices and whole sacrifices
They will offer up whole bulls upon your altar.

For the worship leader
To Mahalath, a maskil of David

The fool said in his heart:
"There is no God"
They corrupted themselves
They performed an abominable evil
There was no one who did good

God looked down from heaven
Upon the children of men
To see if there were any
Who acted wisely
Seeking after God
"They have all been faithless
They have become corrupt
Together
No one does good
Not even one."

"Shall not all who do evil

Be made to know it.

They consume my people

As they consume bread

They do not call upon God."

הֲלֹא יָדְעוּ

פֹּעֲלֵי אָוֶן

אֹכְלֵי עַמִּי

אָכְלוּ לֶחֶם

אֱלֹהִים לֹא קָרָאוּ:

There they feared a fear
Where there was no cause for fear
For God has scattered the bones
Of those that besieged you
You have shamed them
Because God despised them.

Who will bring Israel
Salvation from Sion
When God
Brings his people home
Let Jacob rejoice
Let Israel be glad.

For the worship leader
Set to "Lily of Testimony"
A silent prayer of David. For teaching
When he struggled with Aram-Naharaim and Aram-Jobah
And Joab returned and struck down twelve thousand of Edom
In the valley of salt

O God you have rejected us, broken us
You have been angry, return to us.
You have made the land quake and split it apart
Heal its fractures, for it is breaking up
You have made your people see hard things
You have made us drink the wine of staggering
You have given a banner to those that fear you
Yet let them flee before the bowmen

Selah סֶלָה:
Answer me and save us
That your beloved might be saved
God has spoken
In his holiness:

"I will exult
I will divide up Shechem
I will measure up
The valley of Suceoth
Gilead is mine!
Manasseh is mine!
Ephraim is a helmet
For my head
Judah is my sceptre!
Moab is my washbowl
To Edom I toss my sandal
Over Philistia I will shout!"

אֶעְלֹזָה
אֲחַלְּקָה שְׁכֶם
וְעֵמֶק
סֻכּוֹת אֲמַדֵּד:
לִי גִלְעָד |
וְלִי מְנַשֶּׁה
וְאֶפְרַיִם מָעוֹז
רֹאשִׁי
יְהוּדָה מְחֹקְקִי:
מוֹאָב | סִיר רַחְצִי
עַל־אֱדוֹם אַשְׁלִיךְ נַעֲלִי
עֲלֵי פְלֶשֶׁת הִתְרוֹעָעִי:

Who can take me to a siege proof city?
Who can lead me into Edom?
Is it not you O God who have rejected us
And do not go out with our armies?
Help us against the enemy
For the help of man is empty
In God we can do mighty things
He will trample down our enemies.

For the worship leader a Hymn of David   לַמְנַצֵּחַ מִזְמוֹר לְדָוִד
A song : שִׁיר
In Sion O God silence is praise for you
Vows are fulfilled for you
O hearer of prayer
All flesh comes to you.
Evil things are too strong for me.
You forgive our rebellions.
The happiness of those you choose
And invite to dwell in your courts!
We are sated with the good things of your house
Your holy temple.

In righteousness you answer with awesome deeds, O God of our salvation:
The confidence of the ends of the earth and of the distant seas
Who holds the mountains in place by his strength, who is armed with might
Who stills the raging of the seas, the raging of their waves and the raging of the peoples.
So those who dwell at the ends of the earth will fear your signs.

You will make the gates
Of morning and evening
Shout for joy!

You visit the earth   פָּקַדְתָּ הָאָרֶץ
And make it fruitful   וַתְּשֹׁקְקֶהָ
You heap it with riches   רַבַּת תַּעְשְׁרֶנָּה
The river of God   פֶּלֶג אֱלֹהִים
is full of water   מָלֵא מָיִם
You prepare grain for them   תָּכִין דְּגָנָם
For this   כִּי־כֵן
is how you prepare it   תְּכִינֶהָ
Drenching its furrows   תְּלָמֶיהָ רַוֵּה
Pressing down its ridges   נַחֵת גְּדוּדֶיהָ
Softening it   בִּרְבִיבִים
With abundant showers   תְּמֹגְגֶנָּה
Blessing its growth   צִמְחָהּ תְּבָרֵךְ:

You crown the year of your goodness
And your cart tracks drip with goodness
The pastures of the desert drip with goodness
And the hills clothe themselves with joy

The meadows are clothed with cattle
The valleys are clothed with corn
They shout for joy, yes, they sing!

For the worship leader. A song. A hymn.　　לַמְנַצֵּחַ שִׁיר מִזְמוֹר

Shout to God all the earth
Make music to the glory of his name
Establish the glory of his praise!
Say to God how fearsome are your works
In the greatness of your strength your enemies shrink before you
All the earth shall bow before you
And make music to you
They will make music to your name!

Selah ‏:סֶלָה

Come and see the works of God
How fearsome are his dealings with the children of men
He turned the sea into dried land
They passed through the river on foot
We rejoice in him!
He rules for ever by his power
His eyes keep watch on the nations
Let the rebellious not rise up against him!

Selah ‏:סֶלָה
O peoples bless our God
Let the voice of his praise be heard:

He has held our souls
In life
And not let our foot slip
For you tested us O God
You refined us like
Refined silver
You drew us into the net
You put pressure on us
You let men ride
Over our heads
We went through
Fire and water

שָׂם נַפְשֵׁנוּ
בַּחַיִּים
וְלֹא־נָתַן לַמּוֹט רַגְלֵנוּ׃
כִּי־בְחַנְתָּנוּ אֱלֹהִים
צְרַפְתָּנוּ
כִּצְרָף־כָּסֶף׃
הֲבֵאתָנוּ בַמְּצוּדָה
שַׂמְתָּ מוּעָקָה בְמָתְנֵינוּ׃
הִרְכַּבְתָּ אֱנוֹשׁ
לְרֹאשֵׁנוּ
בָּאנוּ
בָאֵשׁ וּבַמַּיִם

But you brought us out
Into freedom

I will come into your house
With burning sacrifices
I will fulfil my vows to you
Which my lips uttered
Which my mouth spoke
When I was in distress
I will offer a burning sacrifice to you
Of fat cattle
With the sweet smoke of rams
I will prepare bulls and billy goats.

אָבוֹא בֵיתְךָ
בְעוֹלוֹת
אֲשַׁלֵּם לְךָ נְדָרָי:
אֲשֶׁר־פָּצוּ שְׂפָתָי
וְדִבֶּר־פִּי
בַּצַּר־לִי:
עֹלוֹת מֵחִים
אַעֲלֶה־לָּךְ
עִם־קְטֹרֶת אֵילִים
אֶעֱשֶׂה בָקָר עִם־עַתּוּדִים

Selah סֶלָה:

Come and hear
And I will tell
All who fear God
What he has done for me
I cried out to him
With my mouth
And high praise was under my tongue
If I had looked at evil
In my heart
The Lord would not have heard.
But God did hear
He did attend
To the voice of my prayer
Bless God
Who has not
Turned away my prayer
Nor his love from me.

לְכוּ־שִׁמְעוּ
לְכוּ־שִׁמְעוּ
כָל־יִרְאֵי אֱלֹהִים
אֲשֶׁר עָשָׂה לְנַפְשִׁי:
אֵלָיו
פִּי־קָרָאתִי
וְרוֹמַם תַּחַת לְשׁוֹנִי:
אָוֶן אִם־רָאִיתִי
בְלִבִּי
לֹא יִשְׁמַע ׀ אֲדֹנָי:
אָכֵן שָׁמַע אֱלֹהִים
הִקְשִׁיב
בְּקוֹל תְּפִלָּתִי:
בָּרוּךְ אֱלֹהִים
אֲשֶׁר לֹא
הֵסִיר תְּפִלָּתִי
וְחַסְדּוֹ מֵאִתִּי:

73 A Hymn of Asaph   עג מִזְמוֹר לְאָסָף

And yet אַךְ
God is good טוֹב
To Israel לְיִשְׂרָאֵל אלֹהִים
To the clean in heart : לְבָרֵי לֵבָב
But as for me
My feet almost slipped
My step nearly slid
For I envied the arrogant
I saw the peace of the wicked
Their deaths are free of pain
Their bellies are fat.
They have no part in human trouble
They are not touched by human things
So that arrogance is their badge of office
They wear violence like clothes
They narrow their eyes with evil
Dark fantasy flows from their hearts
They mock
They speak malice
They speak oppression
As from on high.
They have enthroned their mouths in the heavens
Their tongue
Walks around the earth.
So people turn to them
And lap up the waters of abundance.
And they say:
'In what way does God know?'
'In the Most High is there knowledge?'

So look
These are the wicked
Always at ease they increase their wealth.
So it was for nothing I kept my heart clean
And washed my hands in innocence
I have been struck down all the day
And my punishment is with me every morning
But if I had said:
'I will speak like this'
Look
I would have betrayed the generation of your sons
So I kept on thinking
How I might understand this
And it was a trouble to my eyes
Until עַד
I came אָבוֹא
Into the sacred places אֶל־מִקְדְּשֵׁי
Of God אֵל־
And understood their destiny אָבִינָה לְאַחֲרִיתָם:

And yet אַךְ
You put them
In slippery places
You throw them
In deceptive ground
In a moment they become a desolation
Entirely destroyed with terrors.
As one waking from a dream
O Lord you arise
And throw off their image.
For my heart was embittered
And I was cut to the quick
I was like a brute
I knew nothing
I was a behemoth before you
Yet I am with you always
You have grasped my right hand
You will guide me with your wisdom
And in the end
You take me up
In glory.
Who but you do I have in heaven?
Having you there is nothing I desire on earth.
My flesh and heart
Come to an end
But God is the rock of my heart
And my portion forever
For look
All who walk away from you perish
You destroy all who break faith with you

But as for me

The closeness of God

Is my

Good

וַאֲנִי

קִרְבַת אֱלֹהִים

לִי־

טוֹב

In the Lord GOD
I have made my shelter
To recount
All your works.

Why O God do you disown us, is it for ever?
Why does your anger smoke
Against the sheep of your pasture?
Remember your people whom you bought in ancient times
The tribe of your inheritance
You have redeemed
Mount Sion where you dwell.
Turn your steps to the everlasting emptiness
All the destruction of the enemy in the holy place
Your adversaries bellow in the midst of your meeting place
They have set up their ensigns for signs.
They seemed like men swinging axes in a tangle of trees
And with axes and hatchets
They hack away all the engraved work.

They set your holy place
On fire
They defiled
The dwelling place
Of your name
In the dust

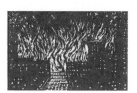

שִׁלְחוּ בָאֵשׁ
מִקְדָּשֶׁךָ
לָאָרֶץ
חִלְּלוּ
מִשְׁכַּן
שְׁמֶךָ :

They said in their hearts:
'Let us suppress them completely'
They have burned every meeting place of God
In the land
We see no signs for us
There is still no prophet.
None among us know how long
How long O God will the adversary taunt?
Will the enemy revile your name forever?
Why do you hold back your hand?
Your right hand?
From the depth of your being
End it כַּלֵּה :

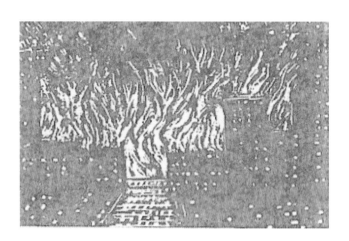

Yet God is my king from the beginning
Making salvation in the midst of the earth
You divided the waters by your strength
You shattered the heads of the river monsters
You crushed the heads of Leviathan
You gave him as food
To the creatures of the desert
You cut open the spring and the wady
You dry up the ever-flowing rivers.
Yours is the day
Yours is the night

You established      אַתָּה הֲכִינוֹתָ:

The moon   מָאוֹר

And the sun   וָשָׁמֶשׁ:

You have set up   אַתָּה הִצַּבְתָּ

All   כָּל

The boundary marks   גְּבוּלוֹת

Of the earth   אָרֶץ

Summer and winter   קַיִץ וָחֹרֶף

You have created

Remember this:
An enemy has taunted
The LORD
A fool people has reviled your name
Do not hand over the life of your turtle dove
To the wild beast
Do not forget your poor for ever
Consider the covenant
For the dark places of the earth
Are full of fields of violence
Do not let the oppressed return humiliated
May the poor and needy praise your name
Arise O God!
Defend your cause!
Remember the daily taunting of the fool
Do not forget the voice of your enemies
The noise of those who rise against you
Rises perpetually.

For the worship leader
In the style of Jeduthun
A Hymn of Asaph

My voice to God: קוֹלִי אֶל־אֱלֹהִים
I shout!   וְאֶצְעָקָה
My voice to God: קוֹלִי אֶל־אֱלֹהִים
Hear me!   וְהַאֲזִין אֵלָי:
In the day of my trouble
I sought the Lord
My hand stretched out in the night
Would not grow numb
My soul refused comfort
I remember God and I groan
I complain and my spirit grows faint.
Selah   סֶלָה:
You hold open the lids of my eyes
I am troubled
I cannot speak
I count up days of old
Ancient years
I remembered my music in the night
I communed with my heart
I search my spirit for answers:
Will the Lord reject us for all time?
Will he never show favour again?
Is his love quite gone forever?
Is his promise void for all generations?
Has God forgotten to be gracious?
Has anger locked up his compassion?
Selah   סֶלָה:
But I say
This is my weakness
Could the right hand of The Most High change!
I will proclaim the deeds of the LORD
I will remember your works of old
I will reflect on your work
I will meditate on your achievements
Your way O God is holiness
What god as great as God?
You are the God who makes wonder
You know your strength among the peoples
You redeem your people with outstretched arm
The sons of Jacob and Joseph
Selah   סֶלָה:

The waters saw you
O God
The waters saw you and churned
Even the depths
Trembled
The thunderheads poured down water
The clouds gave voice
Your arrows flickered around
The voice of your thunder
Is in the whirlwind
The lightnings lit up the world
The earth trembled and quaked

Your path

Is in the sea

Your road

Is in

The great waters

Your footsteps

Are unknown

בַּיָּם

דַּרְכֶּךָ

וּשְׁבִילְךָ

בְּמַיִם

רַבִּים

וְעִקְּבוֹתֶיךָ

לֹא נֹדָעוּ:

You guided your people
Like a flock
By the hand of
Moses and Aaron

O God
The nations have entered your land
They have defiled your holy temple
They have reduced
Jerusalem
To a heap of stones
They have given

The bodies of your servants,
As food for the birds of heaven
The flesh of your beloved ones
To the beasts of the earth
They have poured out blood
Like water
All around Jerusalem
And there is none to bury them
We have become a joke to our neighbours
An object of scorn and derision
To those who surround us.
How long LORD?
Will you be angry forever?
Will your ardour burn like fire?
Pour out your burning anger
Upon the nations that do not know you
Upon the kingdoms
Which do not call on your name
For they have devoured Jacob
And ravaged his pastures
Do not remember our father's guilt

Let your compassion		מַהֵר
Come quickly		יְקַדְּמוּנוּ
To meet us		רַחֲמֶיךָ
For we our brought		כִּי דַלּוֹנוּ
Very low		מְאֹד׃

Help us God of our salvation
For the glory of your name
Deliver us and cover our sins
Because of your name.

Why should the nations say:
'Where is their God?'
Before our eyes
Let there be known among the nations
The requiting
Of the shed blood
Of your servants.
Let the sighs of the prisoner
Come before your face
By the greatness of your arm
Set free
The children of death
And pay back seven times
Into the pocket of our neighbours
The taunts with which they have taunted you
O Lord
And we your people
The sheep you shepherd
Will thank you forever
From generation to generation
We will recount your praise.

85 פה

For the worship leader לַמְנַצֵּחַ
A hymn of the sons of Korah לִבְנֵי־קֹרַח מִזְמוֹר:

LORD
You once favoured your land
You turned back the turning of Jacob
You bore the guilt of your people
And covered all their sins

Selah סֶלָה:

You have gathered up the flowing of your rage
You have turned aside
The burning of your anger
Turn back to us
God of our salvation
And cancel your anger towards us.
Will you be angry with us forever?
Will you drag out your anger
From generation to generation?
Will you not return
And revive us
So your people will rejoice in you?

LORD
Show us your love
And grant us your salvation.
I will listen to what God the LORD
Will say
For he will speak peace to his people
And to his beloved ones
Yet let them not return to folly.
Surely his salvation is close to them that fear him
That glory dwells in our land.

Love and faithfulness
Meet
Righteousness and peace
Kiss
Faithfulness
Springs up from the earth
Righteousness
Leans down
From heaven

חֶסֶד־וֶאֱמֶת
נִפְגָּשׁוּ
צֶדֶק וְשָׁלוֹם
נָשָׁקוּ׃
אֱמֶת
מֵאֶרֶץ תִּצְמָח
וְצֶדֶק
מִשָּׁמַיִם
נִשְׁקָף׃

The LORD will give the good
Our land will give its produce
Righteousness goes before his face
He makes his footsteps a path.

87
Of the sons of Korah
A hymn
A song

פז
לִבְנֵי־קֹרַח
מִזְמוֹר
שִׁיר

His establishment
Is on holy hills
The LORD loves the gates of Sion
More than all the dwellings of Judah
Glorious things are said of you
City of God

Selah סֶלָה:

'I will record Rahab and Babel
As those that know me
Look at Philistia and Tyre
Together with Cush:
"This one was born there!"'

And of Sion (mother)
It will be said
Each and everyone
Is born in her
He
The Most High
Shall establish her
The LORD
Will write
In the register of the peoples
'This one was born there'

Selah ‏סֶלָה‎

So singers as dancers:
'All my springs are in you'.

List of Illustrations

Psalm 1 – i) Tree by water *(wood engraving 1994)*
  ii) Threshing wheat from chaff *(wood engraving 1994)*

Psalm 3 – i) 2 Samuel 17.16 *(wood engraving 1994)*
  ii) 2 Samuel 17.22 *(wood engraving 1994)*

Psalm 4 – i) 2 Samuel 17.4 *(wood engraving 1994)*
  ii) 2 Samuel 17.27, 29 *(wood engraving 1994)*

Psalm 5 – Man and Angel *(wood engraving 1994)*

Psalm 8 – Newton on the beach *(wood engraving 1994)*

Psalm 18 – i) The cords of death *(wood engraving 2020)*
  ii) 2 Samuel 8.14b *(wood engraving 1994)*
  iii) John 20.14 *(wood engraving 1994)*

Psalm 19 – An Angel standing in the sun *(wood engraving 1994)*

Psalm 22 – i) Matthew 27.45 *(wood engraving 1994)*
  ii) Matthew 27.39–43 *(wood engraving 1994)*
  iii) Matthew 27.35 *(wood engraving 1994)*
  iv) The Ninth Hour *(wood engraving 1994)*
  v) Revelation 5.6 *(wood engraving 1994)*
  vi) Matthew 27.50, 51 *(wood engraving 1994)*

Psalm 29 – i) The sons of God *(wood engraving 1994)*
  ii) The Mighty Waters *(wood engraving 1994)*
  iii) The Wilderness *(wood engraving 1994)*
  iv) Mark 4.35–41 *(wood engraving 1994)*

Psalm 30 – i) Death's Door *(wood engraving 1994)*
  ii) Mourning into Dancing *(wood engraving 1994)*

Psalm 38 – The Bed of Sickness *(wood engraving 1994)*